GOD
Power
CHRIST
Power
MASTER
Power

By
Kirpal Singh

An inquiry into the mystery of Christ

A talk delivered on Christmas Day at the St. James Episcopal Church, Houston, Texas, on December 25, 1963.

Includes an appendix "The Essence of Religion"

"The Word of God became man that you also may learn from a man how a man becomes God."

— Clement of Alexandria

I have written books without any copyright—no rights reserved—because it is a Gift of God, given by God, as much as sunlight; other gifts of God are also free.

—from a talk by Kirpal Singh, with the author of a book after a talk to students of religion at Santa Clara University, San Jose, California on November 16, 1972.

The text of this book is the same as what was published during the lifetime of Master Kirpal Singh. Aside from punctuation and capitalization corrections, no changes have been made to the text.

First Edition published in 1964
This Edition published in 2017 by:

RUHANI SATSANG®
DIVINE SCIENCE OF THE SOUL
250 "H" Street, #50
Blaine, WA 98230-4018 USA
www.RuhaniSatsangUSA.org
Tel: 1 (888) 530-1555

ISBN # 978-0-942735-04-8
SAN 854-1906

Printed in the United States of America
by Print Graphics Pros • (949) 859-3845

Sant Kirpal Singh Ji
(1894-1974)

Sawan Singh Ji Maharaj
(1858-1948)

Dedicated

to the Almighty God

working through all Masters who have come

and Baba Sawan Singh Ji Maharaj

at whose lotus feet

the writer imbibed sweet elixir of

Holy Naam — the Word

Sant Kirpal Singh passed on from this earth in 1974. As such, He is no longer taking on new people to guide out of this world and back to God. He left many books that explain, as much as can be in a worldly language, the meaning of life. The books and the Ruhani Satsang website http://www.RuhaniSatsangUSA.org/ are maintained to help stir an interest in God and to help people know what to look for in their search for the way back home.

When asked about a successor, we can only offer this quote from the Master:

> *"Today there is a great awakening beginning. Some have got the answer, some have not, but the search to solve the mystery of life has been born all over the world. The day that question arises in the mind is the greatest day of one's life, for once it is born, it does not succumb until it is satisfied.*
>
> *So, make your life an example of the teachings you follow — live up to them.*
>
> *If you have a strong desire to get it, then God Himself will make the arrangements for you."*

[Excerpts from a talk published in the January 1971 issue of SAT SANDESH]

Dear Friends:

I have the great pleasure to address you on the evening of this day which is considered most sacred among the Christians. Today we are celebrating in sweet remembrance the Christ who appeared at the pole of Jesus.

Thousands of other men are born daily, in all countries, in all towns, but not very many remember their births and deaths; yet the lives of the Masters, so few in number, can never be forgotten.

Christ was born as Jesus. Jesus was the human pole at which the Christ-Power manifested itself, and the Christ-Power never dies. Once that Power takes possession of us under His care, He does not leave us. Christ said, "I am with you always, even unto the end of the world."

When I came here on my last visit in 1955, people asked me, "When is Christ returning?" I asked them, "Has He ever left you?" I quoted to them those very words: "I am with you always, even unto to the end of the world." If He has not left us, then where does the question of coming back arise? The reason we ask these things is because, perhaps, we have not gone far enough into the mystery of Christ.

What was Christ? The God-Power appears from time to time at a human pole to guide the child-humanity and give it the Way back to God. The question is—who can give us the Way back to God? No son of man can do it; God alone can lead us to God or give us a contact with Him. He has no equal — no brother, no father, no mother — and that God resides in every heart.

Thus, have you ever considered who is the one who points the Way back to God and who at times refers to Himself as — "I and my Father are one"; "I am the Light"; "I am the Way."

All Masters tell us that the incarnated Masters are all Children of Light. They are all Sons of God, and whoever follows them meets God, for he is given contact with God. Masters have been coming from time to time, and to all outward intents and purposes, they appear to be men. They were born the same way and their bodies are constructed the same way. What then is the difference between such a Personality and the average man? It is in his being a conscious co-worker of the divine plan, for he sees it is the Father working through him.

Jesus asked his disciples: "What say you that I am?" Simon Peter answered, "Thou art the Son of the living God." Jesus told Peter, "No earthly power has revealed this to you, but my Father which is in heaven." Then again a disciple said that it would suffice if Jesus would show them the Father. What did Jesus reply? He grew indignant and asked, "Have I been so long with you and yet you never saw that it was the Father working through me?" Then he went so far as to say, "Whoever has seen me has seen the Father," and, "No one comes to the Father except by me." These statements are paraphrased from the Bible to make the purpose of them clear.

Christ is the God-Power or so-called Guru-Power, which appeared as the son of man who was called Jesus. During a talk I gave last month at the Unity Temple in Los Angeles, I expressed these thoughts and then asked the minister for his opinion, which I wanted to hear—not because I was doubtful, but because men are evolving and awakening to the truth.

He answered: "Who is Jesus Christ? God's Son, made manifest to man to teach him and to show him the Way and the Truth and the Light. He came to show man how the Father would live if He were a man. He was God in man." Then he explained: "Jesus was the transcendent Incarnation of God." And he continued:"What is the difference between Jesus and the Christ? Christ existed long before Jesus. Jesus is the born man who perfectly manifested the Christ in himself, and Christ is the Divine Nature of this Godman. Thus Christ, the Spiritual Human, existed long before His earthly birth."

Do you comprehend? The Christ-Power or God-Power or Guru-Power is the same, and manifests itself at the human pole to meet the demands of His children: those who feel hungry for Him, those who feel thirsty for Him. There is food for the hungry and water for the thirsty; demand and supply is the law of nature, and where fire burns, oxygen comes to help. When man has hunger for God in his heart, God manifests Himself at some human pole to guide the child-humanity. "No man knows the Father except through the Son and he to whom the Son reveals Him."

As I told you, this Christ-Power existed ever since the world began, and has manifested itself from time to time at the human pole of the various Masters. We can recognize this fact through the study of comparative religions, where we shall find the same teachings given by the Masters of all religions and the same assertions made by them.

Someone told me on my last visit here that Christ is the highest since he had said: "I and my Father are one." "That's all right," I said, "but if other Masters also uttered the same words, how would you consider them?" I then quoted what other Masters had said, in their own languages, in their own times: Guru Arjan, the fifth Guru of the Sikhs, said, "The Son and the Father are dyed in the same color; and the Father and the Son have taken up the same business." The tenth Guru of the Sikhs said, "God ordered me, 'Go—I make you my Son to guide the child-humanity.'" Many others, as well, said the same thing. This is only to prove that Christ lived even before He entered the sinless body of the mother. We have regard for that perpetual Christ-Power which existed before birth and continues after it, and for the Son-ship that is perpetual. That Power lies in every heart and is revealed when a human pole, at which the Power is manifest, meets us and gives us a contact with God. No son of man, no human, can do it, except the manifested God-Power in some human pole.

When we meet them, these human poles are competent to raise our souls from the bondage of mind and the outgoing faculties, and to grant us contact within. Thus, we have regard for all human poles which give that Christ-Power its birth from time to time. We are, then, fortunate that we are gathered here on this blessed Christmas Day.

What is the purpose of the celebration of such birthdays? The aim is to understand the teachings of the Masters, to revive those teachings, and see if we are following them. Blessed be all Masters. We are proud of them; but the question arises—are they proud of us? The true celebration of a great man's birthday is to understand his teachings and live up to them.

II

Christ said, "Because I live, you shall live also." Christ was able to give everlasting life. He referred to himself in our recorded scriptures as: "I am the Bread of Life . . . this is the bread which cometh down from heaven . . . if any man eat of this bread, he shall live forever." God is Light; God is Life; God is Love. What was this Bread of Life he gave?

In another instance, Jesus went to a well to have a drink of water. He requested a Samaritan woman at the well, who was carrying a pitcher of water on her head, to give him some water to drink. Out of an inferiority complex, she said, "You people have no dealings with us; why then are you asking me for water?" Jesus answered, "If you knew who was asking for water, you would have asked for, and I would have given you, the living Water of Life. This water which you carry quenches thirst for a while, yet one is again thirsty; but whoever drinks of the Living Water which I give, will never thirst."

Let us go a little further into it. Who was Christ? (Blessed is the human pole at which Christ appears.) He behaved like a man; he behaved also like God. He behaved like an average man and his greatness lies in this fact. In his grace, he behaved both ways—as a man and as God. St. John describes Jesus as, "The Word was made flesh and dwelt among us."

What is *Word?* Word is definable as "the Word which has made all the heavens." St. John said, "In the beginning was the Word, and the Word was with God, and the Word was God." That is the cause of all Creation. In the Psalms, we find, "Thy Word is settled in heaven." This is what Jesus referred to as the Bread of Life which is come from heaven.

What is that Word, and what is the outer manifestation of the Word which was personified and made flesh in the human pole of Jesus? The Psalmist said, "The Word is a lamp unto my feet, and a light unto my path." Jesus expressly said, "I am the Light of the World."

Do you follow now, how great he was? He was the God-Power manifested in the human pole, and He had great regard for that human pole at which He was manifested; but he always differentiated between the son of man and the God-Father in him. This is no peculiar distinction in the case of Christ, because all other Masters, among them Guru Nanak and Kabir, expounded this same truth in their own languages.

Because we are not aware of the teachings of the other Masters, we think perhaps that the teaching of Jesus is the only truth. Truth, however, is *One*. Truth is clothed in Light. Truth is the Harmony—the Music of all harmonies. The Sikh scriptures contain the same assertion, "The Word was made flesh and dwelt among us," that I quoted to you. They said that the Word was personified in human form and guided the embodied souls and gave them contact back to God. I have respect for all human poles at which that Christ-Power dwells from time to time.

III

You will find very specific teachings from the Masters. They taught first of all, that the highest aim of a man's life is God first, and the world next. We live, however, for the world first and God next; and we have faith in God only insofar as we get worldly things from Him. If sometimes, for some reason or other, we do not receive those things, then our faith is broken.

Jesus said, "Except a man be born again he cannot see the Kingdom of God. . . the Kingdom of God cometh not with observation . . . The Kingdom of God is within you." By observation is meant ways which are related to the outgoing faculties. God is Spirit, and we must pray to God in Spirit alone. God does not reside in temples made by man, but in the God-made temple of the human body. Within that human-body temple, Jesus said, "Because I live, ye shall live also." He did not refer to the outer son of man, the perceptible body, but to the Inner, which gave Light, and was the Way back to God through Love.

God made man after His own image. God is All-Consciousness and Light, and we are also Children of Light. We are conscious entities, environed by mind and matter; and we are kept in the body by the God-Power controlling us. So long as that Power is in the body, we are functioning in it; when that Power is withdrawn, we have to leave it. Similarly, that very Power is controlling the whole universe; and when it is withdrawn, dissolution and grand dissolution set in.

There is a Maker of this universe; it did not just come about by itself. But the Maker Himself is unchangeable, permanent; and the world created by Him, being made of matter, is changing and impermanent.

I would say that the best way to celebrate Christmas Day is to celebrate the lives of these great Lights daily, with every breath. We do not miss or forget the lessons and the teachings they gave us, and we should live up to them daily. We should see the same Christ-Power in ourselves. It is in everyone and it is to be developed through the help given wherever it manifests—call it by any name you like.

Jesus taught that the Kingdom of God could be had only by entering within the human body or the true temple of God. (God is the controlling Power sustaining us in the body.) The import of these teachings is that so long as we are in the body, we are identified with the body and outside things, causing us to forget our inner selves and fall under a grand delusion. How can we be liberated from this delusion?

The attention, which is the outward expression of our soul, is diffused in the world through the outgoing faculties. First we have to withdraw that attention within, and then rise above body-consciousness, above the senses. Only then can we be extricated from the grand delusion that we are the human body instead of being the Indweller of the human body. Only then can we emerge from our ignorance of some higher Power keeping us in the body.

What happens at the time of death? Life withdraws from the extremities and rises to the back of the eyes and then darkness appears. While living, you can learn how to rise above the senses, withdraw from the outside to the back of the eyes, which is the seat of the soul in the body, and have your Inner Eye opened. You can see the Light of God, that Light of God which was personified and called Christ-Power, Guru-Power, or Master-Power.

Jesus told Nicodemus, "Except a man be born again, he cannot see the Kingdom of God." Nicodemus then said, "Lord, I am an old man. How can I enter the womb of the mother and be reborn?" Jesus replied, "Flesh is born of the flesh and spirit of the Spirit."

Our first birth is in the human body; the second birth is that of being born anew into the Beyond when we learn to die while living. This birth is called the Birth in Christ, Birth in Guru-Power, or Birth in God-Power. You must live and die in the God-Power. You must be born in Christ, in the Guru-Power or God-Power. Simply wearing the outer badges of certain schools of thought, or performing specific rites and rituals does not make you be born in Christ. Such practices or beliefs may be the preparation of the ground for being born in Christ, but this birth can be had only if you take up the cross daily. The human body is the cross.

I was very happy to learn from the newspapers today that Pope Paul is making a pilgrimage to Jerusalem. We know that Jerusalem is a place of pilgrimage for all Christians, and perhaps Pope Paul is the first man to go into Jerusalem to revive that memory. I read that he will go down to Jerusalem, take a wooden cross over his shoulders and walk on the ground where Christ walked one day. These things serve to remind us of the great Personalities who came into the world to guide us. Only because Prophet Mohammed was born in Mecca does each Muslim yearn to perform his Hajj or pilgrimage to it. Similarly, we have respect for the birthplaces of all other Masters as reminders to us of their having come. We bow our heads in respect to them, and try to learn the lessons these Masters taught. Unfortunately, these tributes later become conventional and stereotyped social functions, and we forget that the true way to celebrate any great man's life is to understand what he was and taught, to derive the lesson and try to live up to it.

Jesus clearly says that no man knows the Father except the Son, and the one to whom the Son reveals Him. That Son is the Light of God which exists forever. The Son-ship continues. The sum of all that I have to convey to you is that Christ lived as the human body of Jesus, at whose pole

He appeared, and that He resides in every heart. Yet, He cannot be realized by mere feelings, by mere emotions, by merely drawing inferences, or by intellectual wrestling to arrive at a conclusion. It is a matter of seeing God—Who He is. Christ said, "I am the Light of the World." Can you see this Light? Jesus said, "The light of the body is the eye; if therefore thine eye be single, thy whole body shall be full of light."

How can the two eyes be single? This is a practical question and one that can be answered practically, for this occurs when the Inner Eye, which is within each man, is opened. Even a blind man without eyes to see the physical, has that single Eye; but it is closed. We can only see Him, the God-in-action Power, which is the Light called Christ, when we shut the doors of the temple of our body, and our eye becomes single. Our attention has become diffused upon the outside world through the bodily doors of the two eyes, the two nostrils, the two ears, the mouth, the excretory and genital organs; and it has identified itself with them. We have to withdraw our attention from the outside, enter into the laboratory of the human body, which is the true temple of God, and rise to the back of the eyes, where the seat of the soul is located in the body. There lies the tenth door where the eyes become single and where we find the Light of God. There we see the Christ in expression.

This is an example of what I mean by true celebration through the understanding of the Personality of the Master and his teachings, and living up to them.

Jesus said that we must have the Bread of Life and the Water of Life. That Bread of Life and Water of Life lie in the actual contact with the God-into-expression Power of Light and "music of the spheres." At any human pole at which the God-Power is made manifest, that manifested God-Power is competent to raise our souls — bound under mind and outgoing faculties, and identified with them — and open the Inner Eye to see the Light of God, and open the Inner Ear to hear the Voice of God. This is what is meant by coming into contact with the God-into-expression Power of the Light and Sound principle: that is, the true Bread and the true Water of Life. Thus, any human pole at which that God-Power has manifested itself, can give you contact with the Bread and Water of Life.

This is referred to by Guru Nanak and the other Masters who say that we are fortunate to have the human body, and that the purpose of having it is to obtain the Bread of Life and the Water of Life—the true Elixir of Life Everlasting, for whoever drinks of it shall never die.

Remain in any religion you like; but for the Bread and Water of Life, go to a Master who is the human pole of the God-Power or Christ-Power, for no son of man can give you everlasting Life. The greatness of the Master lies not in his advising you how to say prayers or perform certain rites and rituals — any man can give lectures after a little training — but in the fact that he is able to give you a sitting in which your soul is first withdrawn from outside and then raised above the senses; your Inner Eye is opened and you see the Light of God, and your Inner Ear is opened and you hear the Voice of God; and you testify yourself that it is so.

Through the parallel study of religions, you will find the same truth imparted by almost all Masters, in their own languages of course. In the Christian literature, you will find that St. Paul says, "I die daily." Other Masters say: Learn to die a hundred times a day. That death is the withdrawal of the soul from the physical body and rising above it into the Beyond—that is, into the Kingdom of God where you are reborn. "Marvel not that I say unto you, ye must be born again."

These are the teachings given by all Masters from time to time. The difficulty in truly experiencing them, however, lies in the way that our souls are under the command of mind, and mind is under the command of the outgoing faculties. We have abandoned ourselves to the pleasures of the outside world so completely that we have identified ourselves with them, and we remain awake on the outside but asleep from within. You must know that God-Power which is keeping us in the body and, if you are to find this Power, you have to invert and withdraw behind the eyes, and gaze into the dark expanse before you. When you are able to see within that expanse, you will also see the actual God-Power everywhere.

Here is how we can find the Christ already within us. First enter the laboratory of the human body, the true temple of God, then rise above it until we leave all else behind and enter the Kingdom of God. There are so many mansions in the House of our Father; the macrocosm is in the microcosm of the human body, and consists of physical, astral, causal, and super-causal planes; and beyond all these are the pure spiritual planes, the true Home of our Father.

The first step thus starts when we rise and are reborn above the Iron Curtain of this physical body. If anyone can rise above by himself, blessed is he; but if not — consider that even in outward occupations a person needs someone proficient and expert in that particular line — how much more is it necessary to have someone competent where the world's philosophies and outward faculties do not work! Do you not need someone to help you there? You will decide this for yourselves.

In the true terminology of the Saints or Masters, a blind man is defined, not as one who has no eyes on his face, but as one whose Inner Eye is closed. Those who do not see the Light of God are all, excuse me, blind. When they come to a Master and he gives them a sitting, the Inner Eye is opened and they see the Light of God. When they return, they are men with the Inner Eye opened. Similarly, before going to a Master, a man is deaf. When the Master gives him a sitting, he begins to hear the Music of the Spheres and he becomes aware.

These are the gifts of God. The greatness of the Master lies in his competency to give you the Bread and the Water of Life and to help you to be reborn—to open the Inner Eye to see the Light of God, and to open the Inner Ear to hear the Voice of God.

There were few such Personalities in the past, and even now there are few; but the world is not without them. All humanity are the children of these Masters. The same God-Power or Christ-Power has worked ever since the world began, and continues for those children who are hungry and seek the Truth. When that hunger and thirst arises in anyone, God, who resides in every heart, makes arrangements to bring him to wherever he can be duly contacted with his own Self. Can any son of man do it? No. Only the God manifested in him has that Power. Such a person is called a Master.

"Blessed are ye who see things that the old prophets and righteous men could not see, who hear things which the old prophets and righteous men could not hear." These are references in the scriptures that our eyes are sealed and our ears are sealed, and that unless these seals are broken, we cannot see the Light of God and hear the Voice of God.

Guru Nanak was asked, "God resides in every heart, but who can see Him?" He answered, "Those eyes are different, and are other than the eyes of flesh and blood, which can see the Light of God."

Another Saint, Shamas Tabrez, said, "We must be able to see God with our own eyes, and we must be able to hear the Voice of God with our own ears."

The true definition of a Master is given by all Masters as, "one who can make audible for you the Music of the Spheres within, and who can remove the veil of darkness you see when you close your eyes, and reveal the Light of God." Such a person is called a Master.

IV

A life of continence and control over the outgoing senses is enjoined by all Masters as the qualification that enables one to follow their teachings. Jesus said, in the Sermon on the Mount: "Blessed are the pure in heart for they shall see God." All other Masters, or those who have realized themselves, have said the same thing; for God is One and Truth is One. If there are any differences among us, these are all man-made and are due to our lack of personal experience of the Truth. Christ and other Masters have grieved that, although they have seen, although they bear testimony to it, yet the people have not believed them. Masters see and then not only say, but are competent to give us an actual specific experience.

Purity of life is required. You will find that chastity is life and sexuality is death. This body is born of corruptible seed and we are born into the Beyond by the incorruptible seed. We should examine these scriptural references to find their truth. The human body is the highest in all creation and blessed are we that we have it. The highest aim before us is to know God. God resides in us; there is nothing that we need to introduce within from outside.

The various scriptures that we have with us contain a fine record of the experiences of the Masters; yet we need someone who has had this experience and is competent to give it to us — tasting the Bread and drinking the Water of Life — bringing them into existence. Guru Nanak said, "Do not be deluded because you have taken one form of religion or the other. You must follow the original intention of the teachings."

All religious teachings are based on the spiritual experiences of the Masters who came from time to time, and the right import or understanding of these experiences can be had only from those who have had these same experiences. We have due deference for all Masters who came in the past, and great respect for all scriptures, for they are worth tons of gold and emeralds; but we do need someone who knows the Way and can open our Inner Eye to see the Light of God.

The lives of Christ and all Masters are examples of putting God first. The Kingdom of God is within you. You cannot have it by observation; you can have it only by learning to die while alive, for you enter the Kingdom of God only when you are reborn. In the East they say you have to be twice-born, but reborn or twice-born amounts to the same thing. The first birth is in the physical body and the second is into the Beyond. The Masters were competent to give an experience of how to rise above body-consciousness, and gave the *Gayatri Mantra*, meaning to rise above the physical, astral, and causal bodies, to see the Light of the Sun already blazing within you.

As I said before, purity is a stepping stone to Him, and, so is Love of God. Misdirected love, called attachment, is keeping us in the body and is the cause of our coming again and again. We go where we are attached, for that is the nature of attachment. True love, called Charity, is already ingrained in our souls and, when directed towards God, is truly Loving. God is Love, and our soul is Love personified, and the Way back to God is also through Love. All Masters say: Love God with all thy heart, with all thy strength, and love thy neighbor and all creation. On the wings of Love we can fly to heaven—if our lives are chaste.

It is recorded of Christ that he was chaste-born, sinless born. Similarly, in the East, the Masters were the embodiment of chastity and pure lives.

Married life is no bar to spirituality, if conducted according to the scriptures. It means taking a companion in life who will be with you in this earthly sojourn through weal and woe; the husband and wife should help each other to know God and to fulfill the highest aim of man's life. One duty may be that of begetting children, but, bear in mind, it is not 100 per cent of our duties. The scriptures say that husbands should love their wives as Christ loved the church.

In the lives of all Masters, we find two great things: they have contact with God and they are the mouthpieces of God. They speak as inspired from God rather than from the level of the intellect, feelings, emotions, or by drawing inferences. They see and say, and ask you to become. They say: Be still, physically and intellectually, and know that you are God.

We have great respect for all Masters, all sons of men or human poles at which that God-Power, Guru-Power, or Christ-Power worked, and continues to work, to guide child-humanity. We are blessed.

I wish you Happy Christmas, but in the way that I have advocated to be the true celebration of Christmas Day. Understand who the Masters were, their teachings of how to learn to die, how to be reborn, how to open the Inner Eye and see the Light of God. Christ was the Light and the Way.

I have had the great pleasure to present to you for your consideration this Christmas Night, truths which I have come to know through experience and by study of comparative religion.

As I said previously, remain in any religion you like. Unless you sit at the feet of some human pole at which the God-Power has manifested itself, the purpose of your joining various schools of thought has not been served — because you want to *see* God.

The Masters do not destroy any religion or introduce new ones. When they come, it is for the whole world. They consider all humans alike and want us to unravel this mystery of the human body. Great is man. He lives in this body in which God controls him; and within the microcosm of it, exists the macrocosm. We know so much about the outer subjects but, for want of practical people, we know little or nothing about ourselves, and the great boon, the great blessing that we have in the form of the human body — the Golden Opportunity.

Blessed are you. Remain in whatever religion you are, there is no need to change it—but be true to it. And being true to your own religion is, to the best of my knowledge of the scriptures, to sit at the feet of someone who knows the Way.

About the Author:

Considered by many people who met him in the East and in the West to have been a living example of a true Saint of spirituality, Kirpal Singh was born in a rural setting in Sayyad Kasran in the Punjab (then in India, now in Pakistan) on February 6, 1894. He followed the career of a civil servant in the government of India, and retired on his own pension in 1947.

Following instructions from his Master (Sawan Singh Ji Maharaj, 1858-1948), he founded and directed RUHANI SATSANG. He was Commissioned by God and authorized by his Master to carry forward the spiritual work of connecting sincere seekers after God with the WORD (or NAAM). He continued in that capacity until he left the earth plane on August 21, 1974.

Elected four times, consecutively, as President of the World Fellowship of Religions, he upheld the truth that, though the various religions are different schools of thought, the aim of all religions is one and the same. Kirpal Singh visited the major cities in the United States on the occasions of each of his three world tours: in 1955, in 1963-64, and again in 1972, staying in the West for three months or more, each time.

From his study at the feet of Sawan Singh Ji Maharaj and from his own personal inner experiences of a spiritual nature, Kirpal Singh was eminently qualified to convey to sincere people everywhere the importance of self knowledge and God realization.

APPENDIX

The Essence of Religion

This address was delivered by Master Kirpal Singh at the Third World Religions Conference in New Delhi, India on February 26, 1965, in his capacity as President of the World Fellowship of Religions. It was originally published in the May 1971 issue of *Sat Sandesh*.

My own self in the form of ladies and gentlemen:

We have once again gathered together in the historic town of Delhi. This time the Conference of the World Fellowship of Religions, the third of its kind, is being held at a place known as Ramlila Grounds—grounds made hallowed, year after year, by the performance of scenes from the life-story of Lord Rama, who in the ancient epic age symbolized in him the highest culture of Aryavarta, the land of the Aryans. He is worshiped even now as ever before as an ideal in the different phases of life — an ideal son, an ideal brother, an ideal husband and an ideal king, and significantly enough, his life portrays above all the eternal struggle that is going on between virtue and vice, both in the mind of man and in the world around him, leading to ultimate triumph of good over evil.

The idea of World Fellowship of Religions, as you all know, is not a new one. We have had instances of it in the past when enlightened kings like Kharwal, Ashoka, Samudra Gupta,

Harsha Verdna, Akbar and Jehangir held such conferences, each in his own way, to understand the viewpoint of various religions prevailing at the time; and invited the learned men of the realm to translate the scriptures of various religions in the current language of the people. In the present era, the idea was revived when in 1893 a Parliament of Religions was held at Chicago.

The present forum was thought of by Muni Sushil Kumar Ji, who conceived the idea of instituting a World Fellowship of Religions under whose auspices international conferences could be held; and sustained work could be undertaken for promoting mutual respect and understanding of various religions.

Our first Conference was held in November 1957, in the *Diwan-i-Aam*, the Hall of Public Audience in the Red Fort. About three years later, in February 1960, Calcutta became the venue for its deliberations. I am glad that the Fellowship has, during this interval, grown from strength to strength. It is encouraging to see all the delegates that have assembled from the four corners of the earth, representing countless shades of religious thought and opinion, but united in one common endeavor to find out the essential and basic unity of all religions, the common meeting ground where all faiths are one. In short, we are in search of the Grand Truth of Life, the bedrock of all existence, no matter at what level.

All the religions agree that Life, Light and Love are the three phases of the Supreme Source of all that exists. These essential attributes of the divinity that is ONE, though designated differently by the prophets and peoples of the world, are also wrought in the very pattern of every sentient being. It is in this vast ocean of Love, Light and Life that we live, have our very being and move about, and yet strange as it may seem, like the proverbial fish in water, we do not know this truth and much less practice it in our daily life; and hence the endless fear, helplessness and misery that we see around us in the world, in spite of all our laudable efforts and sincere strivings to get rid of them. Love is the only touchstone wherewith we can measure our understanding of the twin principles of Life and Light in us, and how far we have traveled on the path of self-knowledge and God-knowledge.

God is love; the soul in man is a spark of that love, and love again is the link between God and man on the one hand, and man and God's creation on the other. It is therefore said: *He that loveth not, knoweth not God, for God is love*. Similarly, Guru Gobind Singh says: *Verily I say unto thee, that he whose heart is bubbling over with love, he alone shall find God*. Love, in a nutshell, is the fulfillment of the Law of Life and Light.

All the prophets, all the religions and all the scriptures hang on two commandments: *Thou shalt love the Lord thy God with all thy heart, and with all thy soul, and with all thy mind. This is the first and greatest commandment, and the second is like unto it: Thou shalt love thy neighbor as thyself.*

Questioned as to our attitude toward our enemies, Christ said: *Love thine enemies, bless them that curse you, do good to them that hate you, pray for them that despitefully use you and persecute you, that ye may be the children of your Father in heaven. Be ye therefore perfect even as your Father in heaven is perfect.*

With the yardstick of love (the very essence of God's character) with us, let us probe our hearts. Is our life an efflorescence of God's love? Are we ready to serve one another with love? Do we keep our hearts open to the healthy influences coming from outside? Are we patient and tolerant toward those who differ from us? Are our minds coextensive with the creation of God, and ready to embrace the totality of His being? Do we bleed inwardly at the sight of the downtrodden and the depressed? Do the distresses of others distress us? Do we pray for the sick and suffering humanity? If we do not do any of these things, we are yet far removed from God and from religion, no matter how loud we may be in our talk and pious in our platitudes and pompous in our proclamations. With all our inner craving for peace, we have failed and failed hopelessly to serve the cause of God's peace on earth. Ends and means are interlocked things and cannot be separated from each other.

We cannot have peace so long as we try to achieve it with warlike means and with the weapons of destruction and extinction. With the germs of hatred in our hearts, racial and color bars rankling within us, thoughts of political domination and economic exploitation surging in our bloodstream, we are working for wrecking the social structure which we have so strenuously built, and not for peace, unless it be peace of the grave; but certainly not for a living peace born of mutual love and respect, trust and concord, that may go to ameliorate mankind and transform this earth into a paradise for which we so fervently pray and preach from pulpits and platforms, and yet as we proceed, it recedes away into the distant horizon.

Where then lies the remedy? Is the disease past all cure? No, it is not so. "Life and Light of God" are still there to help and guide us in the wilderness. We see this wilderness around us because we are bewildered in the heart of our hearts, and do not see things in their proper perspective. This vast outer world is nothing but a reflex of our own little world within us. The seeds of discord and disharmony in the soil of our mind bear fruit in and around us, and do so in abundance. We are what we think, and see the world with the smoke-colored glasses that we choose to put on. It is a proof positive of one thing only: that we have so far not known the "Life and Light of God," and much less realized "God in man."

We are off center in the game of life. We are playing it at the circumference only, and never had a dip in the deepest waters of life at the center. This is why we constantly find ourselves caught in the vortex of the swirling waters on the surface. The life at the circumference of our being is, in fact, not different from the life at the center of our being. The two are, in fact, not un-identical, yet when one is divorced from the other, they look dissimilar. Hence the strange paradox: the physical life, though a manifestation of God, is full of toil and turmoil, storm and stress, dissipation and disruption. In our enthusiasm and zest for outer life on the plane of the senses, we have strayed too far away from our center, nay, we have altogether lost sight of it; and worse still, have cut the very moorings of our barque and no wonder then we find ourselves tossing helplessly on the sea of life. Rudderless and without a compass to guide our course, we are unwittingly a prey to chance winds and waters and cannot see the shoals, the sandbanks and the submerged rocks with which our way is strewn. In this frightful plight, we are drifting along the onrushing current of life—Where?—We know not.

This world, after all, is not and cannot be so bad as we take it to be. It is a manifestation of the Life Principle of the Creator, and is being sustained by His Light. His Love is at the bottom of all this. The world with its various religions is made for us, and we are to benefit from them. One cannot learn swimming on dry land. All that we have to do is to correctly learn and understand the basic live truths as are embodied in our scriptures, and practice them carefully under the guidance of some theocentric saint.

These scriptures came into being by God-inspired prophets, and as such, some God-intoxicated person or a Godman can give us a proper interpretation of them, initiate us into their right import by reconciling the seeming discrepancies in thought, and finally help us inwardly on the God-path.

Without such a practical guidance, both without and within, we are trapped in the magic spell of forms and minds, and cannot possibly reach at the esoteric truths lying under a mass of verbiage of the bygone ages, and now solidified into fossils with the lapse of time into institutionalized forms, formulae and formularies of the ruling class.

Every religion has, of necessity, a three-fold aspect:

first, the traditional, comprising myths and legends for the lay brethren;

second, the philosophical treatises based on reason to satisfy the hunger of the intellectuals concerned more with the why and wherefore of things than anything else, with great stress on theory of the subject and emphasis on ethical development which is so very necessary for spiritual growth; and

third, the esoteric part, the central core in every religion, meant for the chosen few, the genuine seekers after Truth. This last part deals with the mystic personal experiences of the founders of all religions and other advanced souls. It is this part called *mysticism*, the core of all religions, that has to be sifted and enshrined in the heart for practice and experience.

These inner experiences of all sages and seers from time immemorial are the same, irrespective of the religio-social orders to which they belonged, and deal in the main with the Light and Life of God—no matter at what level—and the methods and means for achieving direct results are also similar.

"Religious experience," says Plotinus, "lies in the finding of the true home by the exile," meaning the pilgrim soul, to whom the Kingdom of God is at present just a lost province. Similarly, Henri Bergson, another great philosopher, tells us, "The surest way to Truth is by perception, by intuition, by reasoning to a certain point, and then taking a *mortal leap*."

These philosophers have said nothing new. They have just repeated, in their own way, the time-honored ancient truths regarding *Para Vidya*, the Knowledge of the Beyond, the references to which, in terse and succinct form, we find in all the scriptures of the world. For example, in Christian theology we have:

i) *Learn to die so that you may begin to live*. And St. Paul significantly adds: *I die daily.*

ii) *He that findeth his life shall lose it, and he that loseth his life shall find it.*

The holy prophet of Arabia speaks of *Mautu Kibal Ant Mautu,* i.e., death before actual death. Dadu and other saints likewise say, *Learn to die while living;* for in the end, of course, everyone has to die.

Thus we have seen that "Life and Light of God" constitute the only common ground at which all religions do meet; and if we could take hold of these saving lifelines, we can become live centers of spirituality, no matter to what religion we owe our allegiance for the fulfillment of our social needs and the development of our moral well-being. God made man, and man, in course of time, made religions as so many vehicles for his uplift according to the prevailing conditions of the people. While riding in these vehicles, our prime need is to raise our moral and spiritual stature to such an extent as to come nearer to God, and this, it may be noted, is not merely a possibility, but as sure a mathematical certainty as two and two make four, with, of course, proper guidance and help from some adept, well versed not only in theory, but also in the practice of the Science of Soul. It is not a province of mere philosophers or theologians or the intellectually great.

I take just two instances to illustrate my point. God, according to all scriptures, is described as the "Father of lights," *Nooran-ala-noor, Swayam jyoti sarup,* all of which are nothing but synonymous terms. But ask any religious authority as to the connotation of these words and he would say that these are only figurative terms without any inner significance. Why? Because he has not actually experienced in person His Light, un-create and immortal, self-effulgent and shadowless, which Moses, Zoroaster, Buddha, Christ, Mohammed, Nanak, Kabir and others of their kind actually witnessed and realized, and taught those who came in contact with them to do likewise.

Again, like the practice of lighting candles (symbolic of the inner light), there is another practice of ringing the bell or bells in churches and temples and giving of *Azaan* by *Mouzan* which has a much deeper inner significance than is realized, and surprisingly enough is taken to be just a call to the faithful for prayer. Herein lies the great hiatus between learning and wisdom, which are at poles asunder; for this too is symbolic of the music of the soul, the Audible Life

Stream, the music of the spheres, the actual life principle pulsating in all the creation.

Without taking any more of your time, I would like to emphasize one thing: that all religions are profoundly good, truly worthy of our love and respect. The object of this Conference is not to found any new religion as we have already enough of them, nor to evaluate the extant religions we have with us. Again, we should shed the idea of drawing up "One World Religion"; for all religions, like so many states, are, in spite of their variegated forms and colors, but flowers in the garden of God, and smell sweet.

The most pressing need of the time, therefore, is to study our religious scriptures thoughtfully, and to reclaim our lost heritage. *Everyone has in him,* says a Saint, *a pearl of priceless value, but as he does not know how to unearth it, he is going about with a beggar's bowl.* It is a practical subject and even to call it a religion of soul is a misnomer, for soul has no religion whatsoever. We may, if you like, call it the Science of Soul, for it is truly a science, more scientific than all the known sciences of the world, capable of yielding valuable and verifiable results, quite precise and definite. By contacting the Light and Life Principles, the primordial manifestations of God within the laboratory of the man body, (which all the scriptures declare to be a veritable temple of God), we can virtually draw upon the "bread and water of life," rise into Cosmic Awareness and gain immortality.

This is the be-all and end-all of all religions, and embedded as we all are in the *One Divinity;* we ought to represent the noble truth of the Fatherhood of God and the brotherhood of man. It is the living Word of the living God, and has a great potential in it. It has been rightly said: *Man does not live by bread alone, but by the Word of God.* And this Word of God is an unwritten law and an unspoken language. He, who by the power of the Word, finds himself, can never again lose anything in the world. He, who once grasps the human in himself, understands all mankind. It is that knowledge by knowing, which everything else becomes known.

This is an immutable law of the Unchangeable Permanence and is not designed by any human head. It is the *Sruti* of the Vedas, the *Naad* or *Udgit* of the Upanishads, the *Sraosha* of the Zend Avesta, the *Holy Spirit* of the Gospels, the lost *Word* of the Masons, the *Kalma* of the Prophet Mohammed, the *Saut* of the Sufis, the *Shabd* or *Naam* of the Sikh scriptures, the Music of the Spheres and of all harmonies of Plato and Pythagoras, and the Voice of the Silence of the Theosophists. It can be contacted, grasped and communed with by every sincere seeker after Truth, for the good not only of himself but of the entire humanity; for it acts as a sure safety valve against all dangers with which mankind is threatened in this atomic age.

The only prerequisite for acquiring this spiritual treasure, in one's own soul, is self-knowledge. This is why sages and seers, in all times and in all climes, have in unmistakable terms laid emphasis on self-analysis. Their clarion call to humanity has always been: *Man—Know Thyself.* The Aryan thinkers in the hoary past called it *Atam Gian* or knowledge of the Atman or soul. The ancient Greeks and Romans, in turn, gave to it the name of *gnothi seauton* and *nosce teipsum,* respectively. The Muslim divines called it *Khud-Shanasi;* and Guru Nanak, Kabir and others stressed the need for *Apo Cheena* or self-analysis; and declared that so long as a man did not separate his soul from body and mind, he lived only a superficial life of delusion on the physical plane of existence. True knowledge is undoubtedly an action of the soul, and is perfect without the senses. This then is the acme of all investigations carried out by man since the first flicker of self-awakening dawned in him.

This is the one truth I learned in my life, both in theory and practice, from my Master, Baba Sawan Singh Ji Maharaj, and have today placed it before you, as I have already been doing before the peoples in the West and East during my extensive tours all over; and have on experience found it of ready acceptance everywhere as a current coin; for it is the sole panacea for all the ills of the world, as well as ills of the flesh, to which man is a natural heir through the working of the inexorable law of action and reaction—*ye shall reap, as ye shall sow.*

All of our religions are, after all, an expression of the inner urge felt by man, from time to time, to find a way out of the discord without into the halcyon calm of the soul within. The light shineth in the darkness and the darkness comprehendeth it not. But we are so constituted by nature that we feel restless until we find a rest in the Causeless Cause. If we live up to our scriptures, and realize the Light and Life of God within us, then surely, as day follows the night, Love would reign supreme in the Universe, and we will see nothing but the Unseen Hand of God working everywhere.

We must then sit together as members of the One Great Family of Man so that we may understand each other. We are above everything else, ONE—from the level of God as our Father, from the level of Man as His children, and from the level of worshipers of the same Truth, or Power of God, called by so many names. In this august assembly of the spiritually awakened, we can learn the "Great Truth of Oneness of Life" vibrating in the Universe.

If we do this, then surely this world, with so many forms and colors, will appear a veritable handiwork of God, and we shall verily perceive the same life-impulse enlivening all of us. As His own dear children embedded in Him, like so many roses in His rose bed, let us join together in sweet remembrance of God, and pray to Him for the well-being of the world, in this hour of imminent danger of annihilation that stares us in the face. May God, in His infinite mercy, save us all, whether we deserve it or not.

Before I sit down, I heartily welcome you, my brothers and sisters, and thank you warmly for your kindness and sincerity in furthering such a noble mission that has brought us together.

BOOKS by Kirpal Singh

CROWN OF LIFE: A Study in Yoga
The ultimate aim of all yoga, at-one-ment with the Supreme Lord, is the focusing point of this study of comparative yoga. All the important forms, ancient and modern, are taken up in turn, their practices explained and discussed, and the extent to which each can lead us toward the final goal is evaluated. The standard for comparison is *Surat Shabd Yoga*, the Crown of Life, the highest form of Yoga. Religious parallels and various modern movements are cited. 384 pages, index.
Soft Cover ISBN 978-0-942735-77-2
Hard Cover ISBN 978-0-942735-75-8

GODMAN
If there is always at least one authorized spiritual guide on earth at any time, what are the characteristics which will enable the honest seeker to distinguish him from those who are not competent? This book is recommended to seekers looking for a successor to Kirpal Singh — a complete study of the supreme mystics and their hallmarks.
Soft Cover ISBN 978-0-942735-64-2, 250 pages
Hard Cover ISBN 978-0-942735-70-3, 196 pages

A GREAT SAINT: BABA JAIMAL SINGH
His Life and Teachings
A unique biography, tracing the development of a true Saint [1838-1903]. Should be read by every seeker after God for the encouragement it offers. Also included: *A Brief Life Sketch of Hazur Baba Sawan Singh*. As the successor to Jaimal Singh, Sawan Singh [1858-1948] carried on the spiritual work, greatly expanding the Sangat in the East and in the West. Soft cover, 246 pages, glossary, index. ISBN 978-0-942735-27-7

HIS GRACE LIVES ON
During 17 days in August 1974, preceding His physical departure on August 21st, Kirpal Singh gave 15 darshan talks, mostly in the form of questions and answers, to a small group of disciples at His ashram in India. Also included is the text from His August 1974 address to the Parliament of India, and the 1971 darshan talk, *True Meditation*.
Hard cover ISBN 978-0-942735-93-2
Soft cover ISBN 978-0-9764548-3-0, 208 pages.

THE JAP JI: The Message of Guru Nanak
An extensive explanation of the basic principles taught by Guru Nanak [1469-1539] with comparative scriptures cited. The translator presents a literal translation of the Punjabi text [also included] with an introduction and commentary. Also includes a biographical study of Guru Nanak. Soft Cover ISBN 978-0-942735-81-9, 287 pages.
Hard Cover ISBN 978-0-942735-85-7, 208 pages.

THE LIGHT OF KIRPAL [Heart to Heart Talks]
A collection of 87 talks given from September 1969 to December 1971, containing extensive questions and answers between the Master and western disciples visiting His ashram in India at that time. [A slightly different version of this book was published under the title *Heart to Heart Talks.*] Soft cover, 446 pages, 15 photos. ISBN 978-0-89142-033-0

MORNING TALKS
A transcription of a series of talks given by Kirpal Singh between October 1967 and January 1969. "My new book *Morning Talks*,...which covers most aspects of Spirituality, is a God-given text-book to which all initiates should constantly refer, to see how they are measuring up to the standards required for success in their man-making. I cannot stress sufficiently the importance of reading this book, digesting its contents, and then living up to what it contains." Soft cover, 264 pages. ISBN 978-0-942735-16-1

NAAM or WORD
"In the beginning was the WORD. . . and the WORD was God." Quotations with commentary from Hindu, Buddhist, Islamic, Christian and other sacred writings confirm the universality of this spiritual manifestation of God in religious tradition and mystical practices. 480 pages.
ISBN 978-0-942735-94-9. Soft cover.
ISBN 978-0-942735-90-1. Hard cover.

THE NIGHT IS A JUNGLE — 14 talks from *Sat Sandesh*
The first four talks cover the whole range of spiritual teachings. The following talks explain in detail the necessity of a Master, the role of the Master on Earth, the changes that must take place within the disciple, and how to overcome difficulties on the Path. The final discourse explains how the busy householder can reach the final goal without leaving his work and family by making the nights his "jungle". Soft cover, 368 pages, with an introduction.
ISBN 978-0-942735-18-5

PRAYER: Its Nature and Technique
"True prayer consists of withdrawing the spirit within with a pure mind and fully devotional attitude. Such a prayer cannot but bear fruit in abundance and in no time." Discusses all forms and aspects of prayer, from the most elementary to the ultimate state of "praying without ceasing." Also includes collected prayers from all religious traditions and the talk *Simran* as appendices. ISBN: 978-0-942735-50-5 Soft cover, 978-0-942735-51-2 Hard cover, 246 pages.

SPIRITUAL ELIXIR
Collected questions addressed to Kirpal Singh in private correspondence, together with respective answers organized by topic. Also includes various messages given on special occasions. Soft cover, 382 pages, glossary.
ISBN 978-0-942735-02-4

SPIRITUALITY: What It Is
A straightforward explanation of man's ultimate opportunity – Spirituality, the science of developing higher consciousness in man at the level of the soul, and making one transcend from mere body consciousness into Cosmic and then Super Consciousness, so as to enable one to understand the working of the Divine Plan.
Soft cover, 192 pages. ISBN 978-0-942735-78-9

SURAT SHABD YOGA (Chapter 5 of *Crown of Life*)
The Yoga of the Celestial Sound Current is a perfect science; it is free from the drawbacks of other yogic forms. Emphasis is placed on the need for a competent living Master. This book is an excerpt from the larger book *The Crown of Life*, and is an excellent short but complete explanation of the Path of the Masters. Includes a brief life sketch of Sant Kirpal Singh.
Soft cover, 86 pages. ISBN 978-0-942735-95-6

THE TEACHINGS OF KIRPAL SINGH
Definitive statements from various talks, books and letters by the author, reorganized by topic to illuminate the aspects of self-discipline pertinent to Spirituality. Relevant questions are answered. This collection allows the reader to research by topic.
Complete set in one book ISBN 978-0-942735-33-8, 512 pages

THE WAY OF THE SAINTS
Collected short writings of Sant Kirpal Singh, including some of the booklets, circular letters, and seasonal messages. Included is a brief biography of Baba Sawan Singh, the author's Master, plus many pictures.
Paperback; 402 pages. ISBN 978-0-89142-026-2

THE WHEEL OF LIFE & THE MYSTERY OF DEATH
Originally two separate books, now bound in one volume. When you sow a seed, it will bring forth similar seeds. There is action-reaction, then again a reaction; there is no end to it. The meaning of one's life on earth and the Law of Karma [the law of action and reaction] are examined in *The Wheel of Life*. In *The Mystery of Death*: They [the Masters] point out and demonstrate to us the way to conquer the seemingly invincible and terrifying death and thus become fear-free....and ultimately rise to realize our divine nature and see oneness in God – the All-consciousness and bliss. Soft cover, 320 pages
ISBN 978-0-942735-80-2

THE THIRD WORLD TOUR OF KIRPAL SINGH
This book was printed directly from the pages of *Sat Sandesh* magazine, the issues from October 1972 through February 1973, which were primarily devoted to Master Kirpal Singh's Third World Tour. 160 pages, 80 black and white pictures.

BOOKLETS by Kirpal Singh

GOD POWER / CHRIST POWER / MASTER POWER
Discusses the ongoing manifestation of the Christ-Power and the temporal nature of the human bodies through which that Power addresses humanity. "Christ existed long before Jesus." Includes the appendix "The Essence of Religion". Soft cover, 44 pages.
ISBN 978-0-942735-04-8

HOW TO DEVELOP RECEPTIVITY
Five Circular Letters concerning the attitudes which must be developed in order to become more spiritually receptive. Soft cover, 60 pages, ISBN 978-0-942735-10-9

MAN! KNOW THYSELF
A talk especially addressed to seekers after Truth. Gives a brief coverage of the essentials of Spirituality and the need for open-minded cautiousness on the part of the careful seeker. Originally published in 1954. Soft cover, 38 pages, ISBN 978-0-942735-06-2

RUHANI SATSANG: Science of Spirituality
Briefly discusses "The Science of the Soul"; "The Practice of Spiritual Discipline"; "Death in Life"; "The Quest for a True Master"; and "Surat Shabd Yoga." Soft cover, 36 pages.
ISBN 978-0-942735-03-1

SEVEN PATHS TO PERFECTION
Describes the seven basic requisites enumerated in the prescribed self introspection diary which aid immeasurably in covering the entire field of ethics, and help to invoke the Divine Mercy. Includes Circular 17 and a letter to an initiate as appendices. Soft cover, 46 pages. ISBN 978-0-942735-07-9

SIMRAN: The Sweet Remembrance of God
Discusses the process of centering the attention within by repeating the "Original or Basic Names of God" given by a True Master. Originally published in 1954. Soft cover, 48 pages ISBN 978-0-942735-08-6

THE SPIRITUAL AND KARMIC ASPECTS OF THE VEGETARIAN DIET
An overview of the vegetarian diet containing a Circular Letter from Kirpal Singh on the spiritual aspects, a letter from Sawan Singh on the karmic aspects, and excerpts from various books by Kirpal Singh. Soft cover, 50 pages. ISBN 978-0-942735-47-5

Material of Master Kirpal Singh can be ordered from this address, by phone or online.

RUHANI SATSANG®
250 "H" St. #50, Blaine, WA 98230-4018 USA
Phone 1-888- 530-1555, Fax 1-604-530-9595
Website: www.RuhaniSatsangUSA.org
Email: RuhaniSatsangUSA@gmail.com